IN MAD® WE TRUST!

by
SERGIO ARAGONÉS

**ALBERT B.
FELDSTEIN,
Editor**

W9-BGR-302

**WARNER
PAPERBACK
LIBRARY**

A Warner Communications Company

WARNER PAPERBACK LIBRARY EDITION
First Printing: March, 1974

Copyright © 1974 by Sergio Aragonés
and E.C. Publications, Inc.

This Warner Paperback Library Edition is published by arrangement
with E.C. Publications, Inc.

**Warner Paperback Library is a division of Warner Books, Inc.,
75 Rockefeller Plaza, New York, New York 10019.**

W A Warner Communications Company

a mi mamá

A HAREBRAINED IDEA

SUBSTITUTE TEACHING

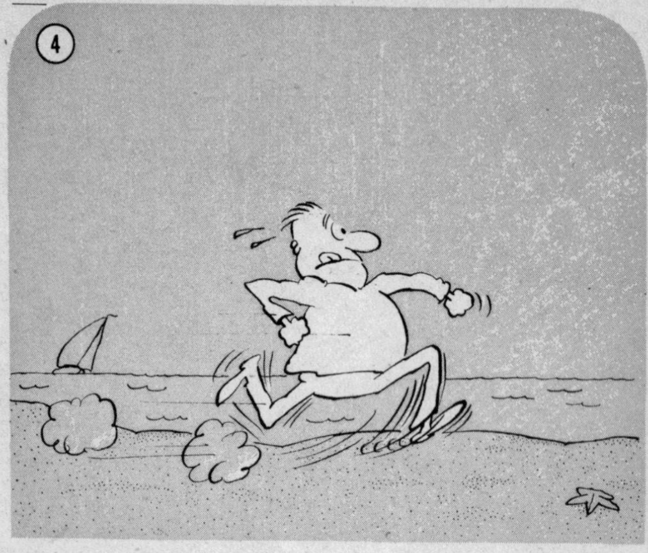
4

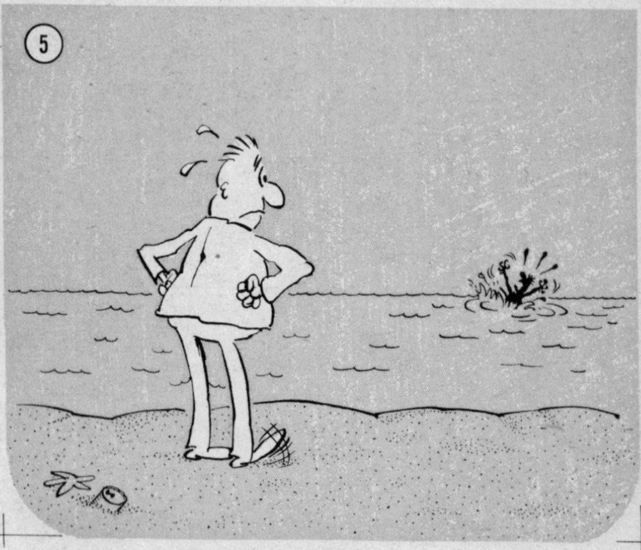
5

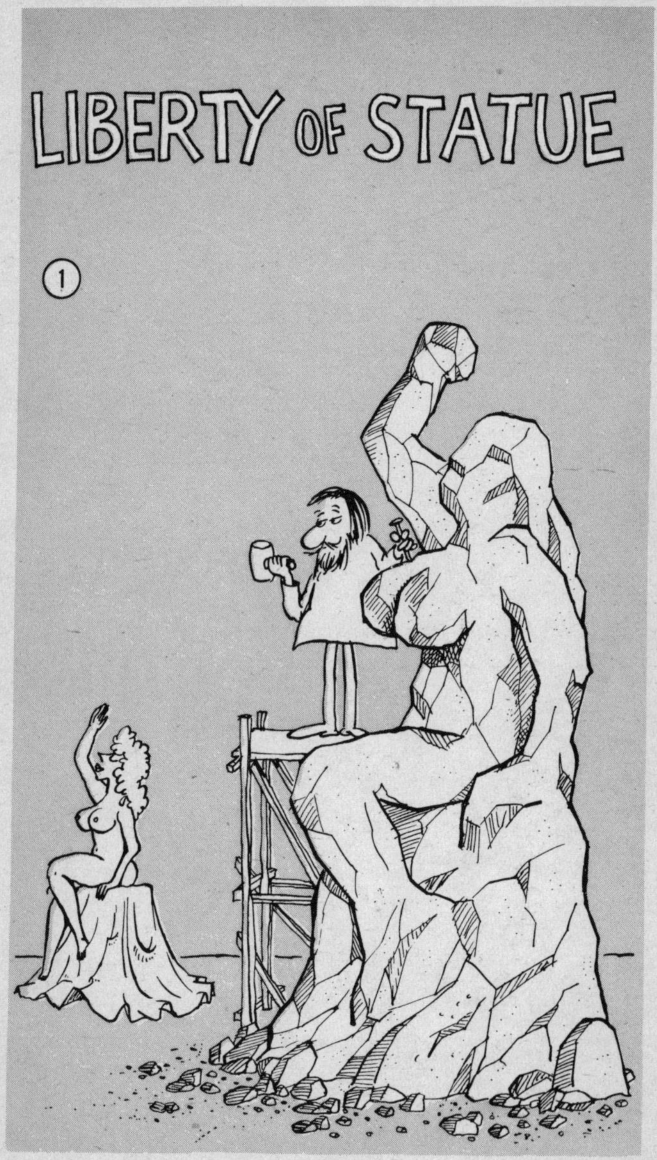

LIBERTY OF STATUE
1

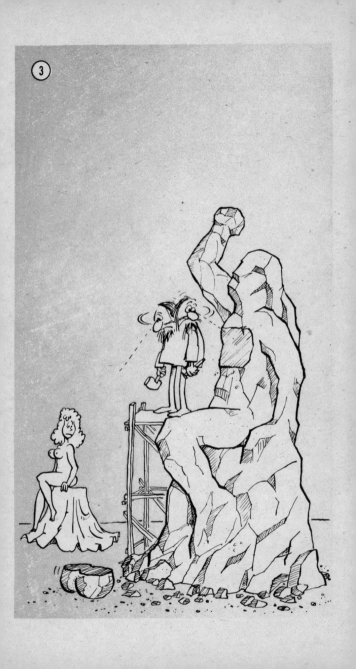

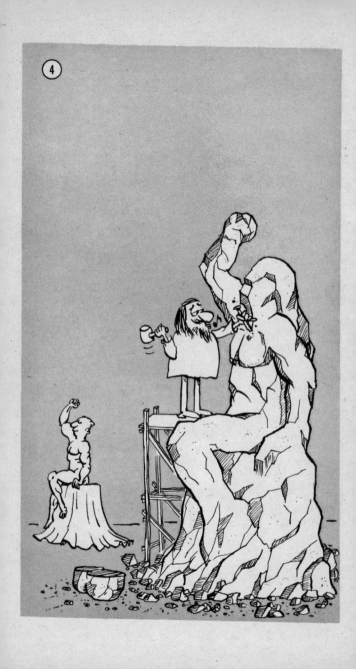

QUICK ON THE RIGGER!

HEX MARKS THE SPOT

A BALANCED ACCOUNT

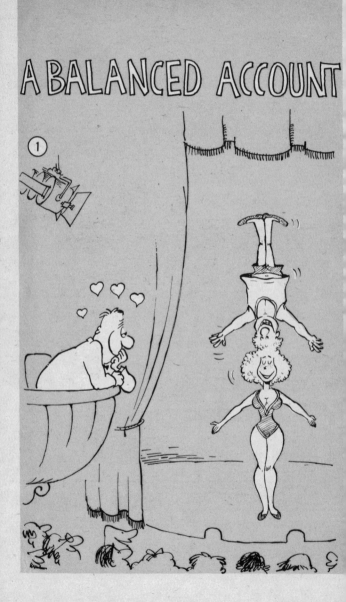

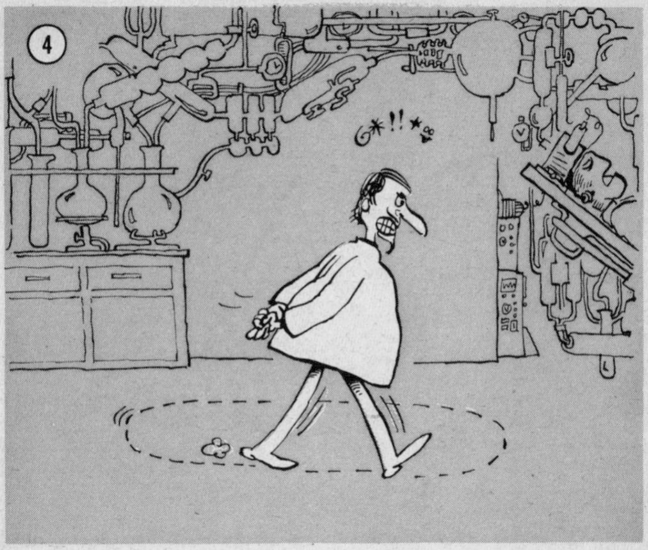
4
G*!!*

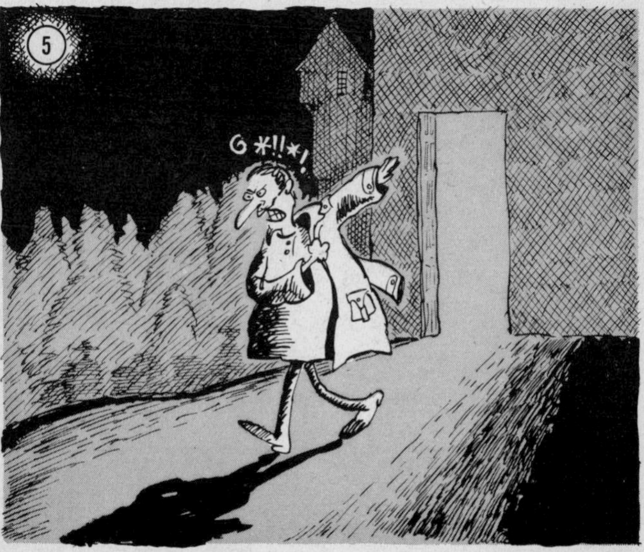
5
G*!!*!

ATTENTION, PLEASE!

①

IN QUEST OF THE HUIZINETZAPOPIXTLAXOCHI IDOL

A REVOLUTIONARY IDEA..

THE
RESOLUTION

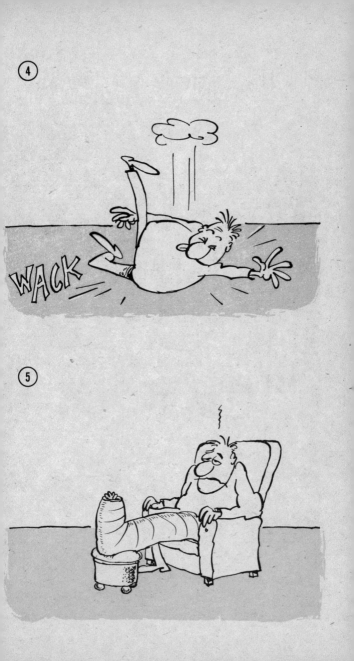

HORSE
MANEUVER

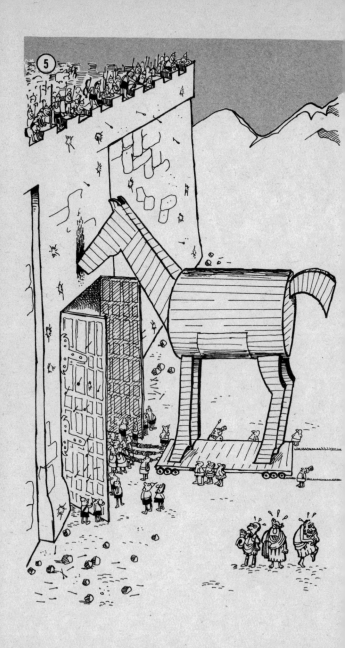

CHILD'S PLAY

ONE FOR THE ROAD!

①

ORAL GRATIFICATION

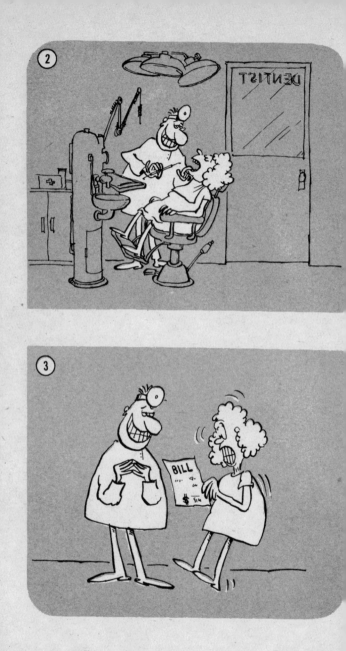

A BEASTLY ACT

SNOW JOB

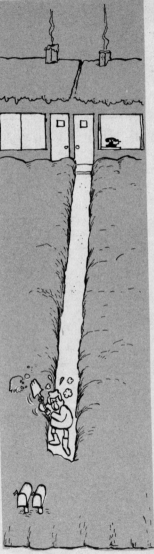

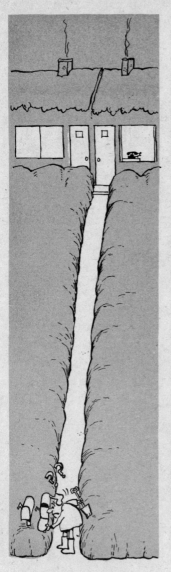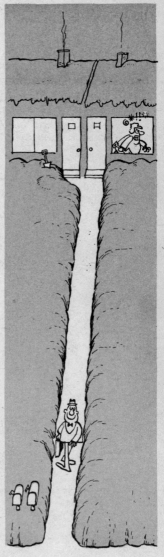

PHOTO-FINISH

①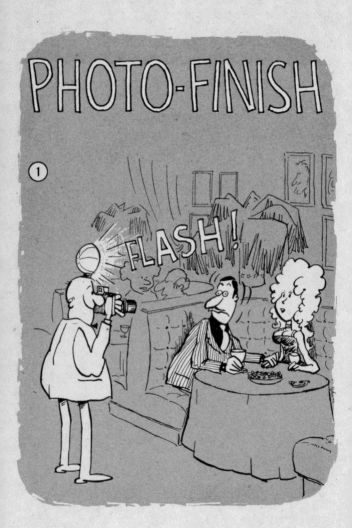

STP ALL OVER THE PLACE!

A GRIZZLY PROPHECY

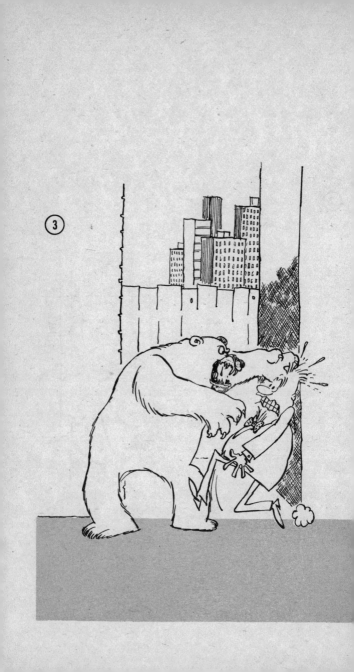

THE CUSTOMER IS ALWAYS RIGHT!

INDIAN GIVER

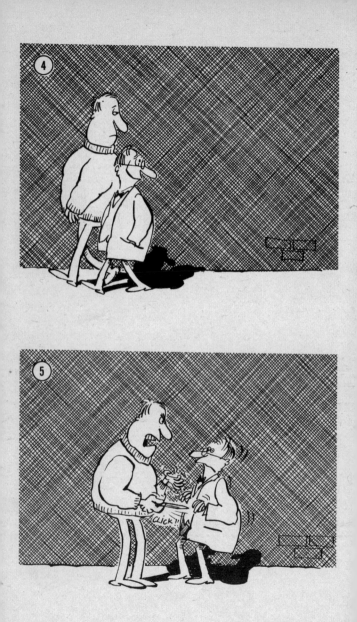

THE
BLACKBOARD BUNGLE

MATERIAL WITNESSES

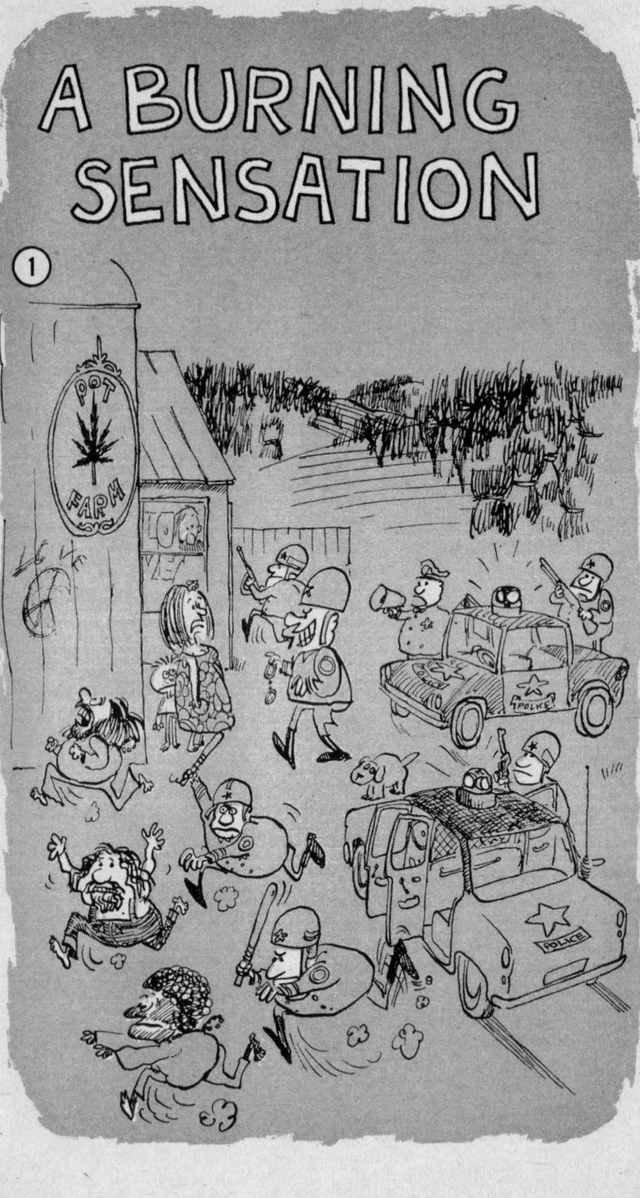
A BURNING SENSATION
1
POT FARM
POLICE
POLICE
POLICE

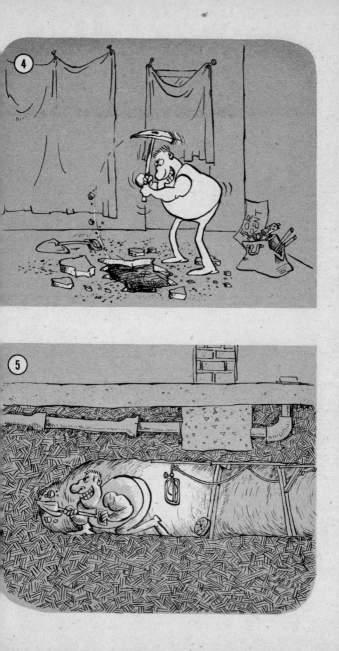

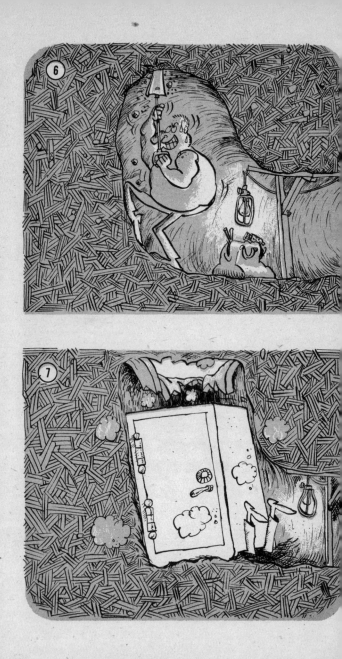

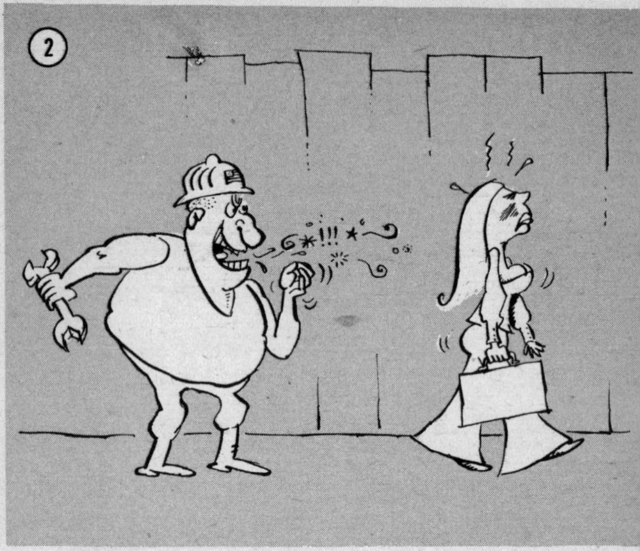
2

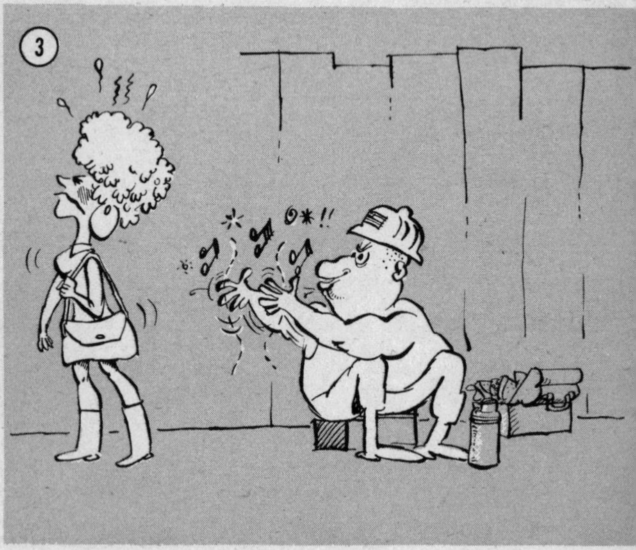
3

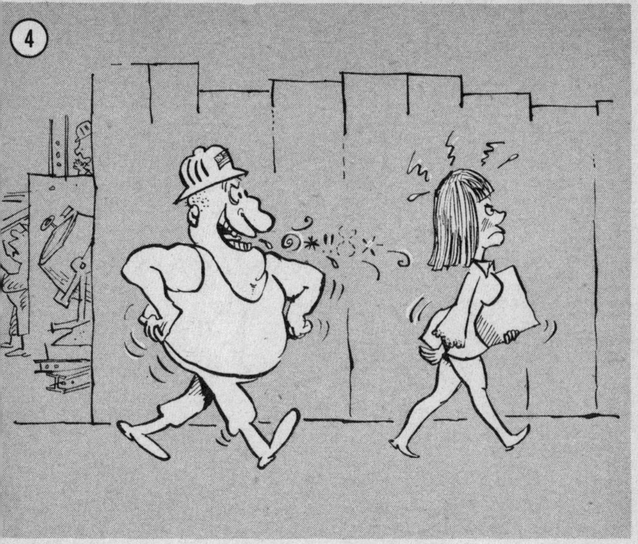
4

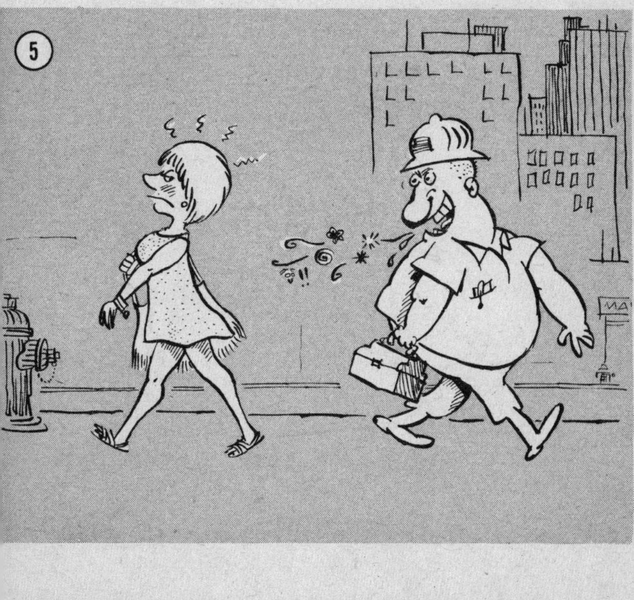
5

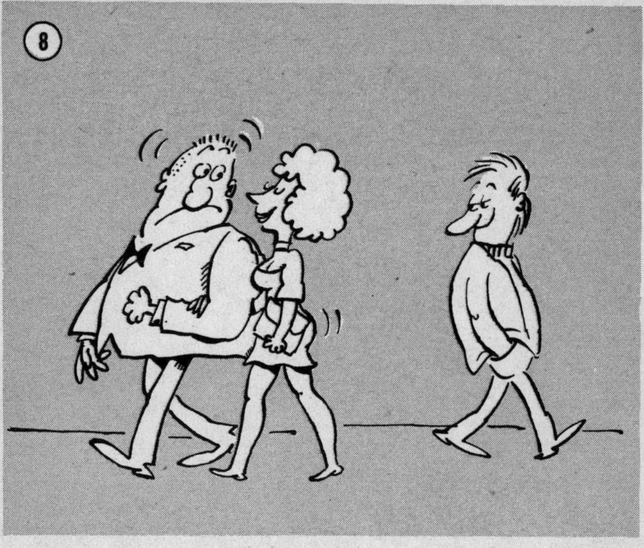
8

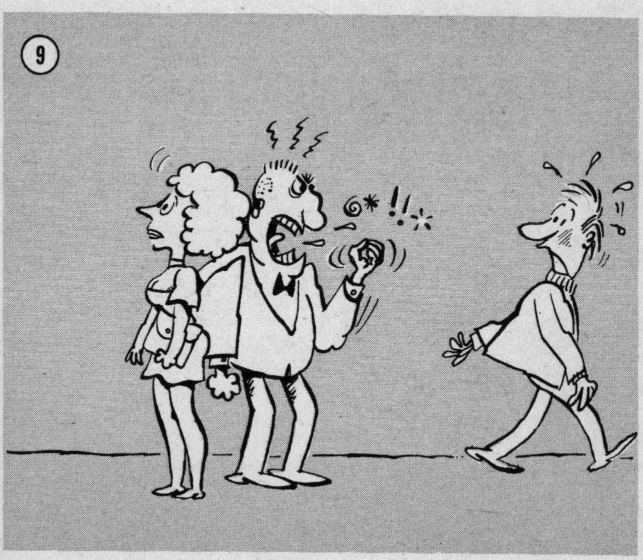
9

DIAPER SERVICE

FIGURE IT OUT!